ST. GEORGE

1. The Globe Picture Theatre in Church Road, on the corner with Jane Street, the films showing were a double bill, *"The Lion Cubs"* and *"My Old Dutch"*. The adjoining shop was Davies and Son, Butchers.

2. Redfield Wesleyan Chapel opened on April 8th 1884, by the Rev. Thos. McCullagh. It is built in Gothic style of architecture of Pennant Stone. Situated in Church Road on the corner with Gilbert Road, today it is a Church Shee Sanatan Deevva Mandel.

ST. GEORGE

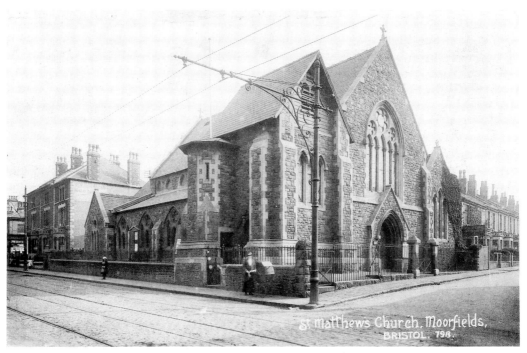

3. St. Matthew Moorfields, this church was consecrated by Bishop Ellicott on January 28th 1873, and since that date has been considerably enlarged. Situated adjoining Church Road in Cowper Street. Postcard postally used in 1911.

4. A procession of choir boys wending their way along Cowper Road from the Parish Rooms for a service in St. Matthews Church to celebrate the re-opening of the church in 1907.

5. Church Road from the corner with Victoria Road towards St. Georges Park. A galvanised bath can be seen hanging from the first shop, a hardware store, with Redfield Post Office further along, c.1905.

6. This close-up view shows the wide variety of shops including drapers and furnishers. Many of the upper facades remain the same today. The postcard was produced by J.C. Young and posted to Dawlish in August 1908.

7. Witchell Road double bay terraced houses between Church Road and connecting at the far end with Victoria Ave. c.1908.

8. Hamilton Terrace, a row of terraced houses in Church Road. It is suggested that these houses were built on a mound of red earth, hence the name Redfield. This postcard was postally used in 1908.

9. Roseberry Road, c.1910, with neat double bay villas connecting with Baden Road and Avon Vale Road.

10. The corner shop in Avon Vale Road, the proprietor Mr. J.W. Harris, Ironmongers. The signs are advertising Puritan Soap and Royal Daylight Lamp Oil. The shop on the corner with Roseberry Road is today converted into a private house.

11. Leonard Road, a turning off of Avon Vale Road, and connecting with Weight Road. It continues round past Avonvale Schools into Victoria Avenue.

12. Victoria Parade as it is known today, in this view c.1908, it was known as Victoria Street. This view is from the Whitehall Road end near the corner with Clare Street.

13. The Providence Meeting Room in Whitehall Road on the corner with Herbert Street, with shops either side. This postcard was postally used in 1906.

14. A close view of the Providence Meeting Room, number 145 Whitehall Road, showing the stepped entrance and lamp above. It was built in 1898.

15. Gilbert Road from the Whitehall Road end c.1908. Children standing around informally for the photographer.

16. Neath Road, a mixture of double bay villas. The road is off of Whitehall Road, and joins Whitehall Gardens near the Packers Playing Fields.

17. Stanley Gerrish, Market Gardener, lived at Bellevue House, 88 Gordon Road. This view of his gardens in St. George in 1913. This postcard written by Mr. Gerrish ordering beans from a Mr. Hazell, at 10/- (50p) a cwt, to be delivered in ½ cwt bags!

18. Speedwell Road showing red brick council houses, built to ease the housing shortage in the 1920's and early 1930's, looking towards Kingswood.

19. Beaufort Road, with Richmond Road the turning on the right. This road faces Avon View Cemetery, and connects Blackwarth Road and The Avenue near Summerhill Road.

20. Salisbury Street, a view on a summers day, the left side is in shadow. These terraced houses connect with Beaufort Road, and join the main road at Church Road.

21. Avon View Cemetery showing the Mortuary Chapel, with its neat flower beds and unusual trim to the evergreen tree in the foreground.

22. A family about to visit Avon View Cemetery waiting at the gates. The Chapel and the clipped tree of illustration 21, behind the entrance gates.

23. Lambley Road with St. Georges Church at the far end, c.1908. The church was demolished in 1976. Since then houses and flats have been built by Bristol Church Housing Association on the site.

24. A closer view of the double bay villas in Lambley Road, from the end which joins with The Avenue and Beaufort Road. An unusual feature of these houses are the individual names of each house carved in the stone between the two bays.

25. St. Georges Higher Grade School, opened in 1894, was founded by local shopkeepers, and a local Minister, at a cost of £14,000. The first headmaster was Mr. G.W. Westaway.

26. Below St. Georges Higher Grade School, is a Victorian iron toilet, and next door to the house a shoeing forge, owned by Mr. Frederick G. Snellgrove. This postcard c.1905.

27. A class of boys studying in the Chemistry Laboratory. These boys came from a large catchment area, including the Feeder canal by the cotton works, through to the White Swan in Stapleton Road, across to Cossham Hospital, including parts of Kingswood and Conham Vale.

28. The School included both boys and girls, this picture shows girls absorbed in experiments with the aid of scales.

29. A group of older boys and girls outside the school. The master with the moustache is Mr. J.W. Watson, who joined the staff of St. Georges Higher Grade School when the school first opened on November 15th 1894. The first pupils attended on Monday November 19th 1894.

30. This view of St. Georges Higher Grade School is taken from the back, in St. Georges Park. When the school opened it was the first Higher Grade School in the country.

31. This ornate iron drinking fountain at the entrance to St. Georges Park, which is near the junction with Chalks Road and Church Road. A delightful group of children are gathered around the fountain, c.1914.

32. St. Georges Park was first opened in 1894. This view c.1913 shows a well laid-out park with a boating lake. The large building on the skyline belonged to the Bristol Co-operative Society Ltd.

33. Park Crescent facing St. Georges Park, situated between Lake View Road and Howard Street. The postcard was postally used on December 23rd 1909 from no.58, with Christmas Greetings and finishes with *"X is where our house is"*!

34. Lyndale Road, a turning off of Chalks Road. These terraced houses face St. Georges Park, with St. Georges School on the far side of the park, c.1908.

35. Church Road continuing from St. Georges Higher Grade School, out of the city. The turning on the right is Seneca Street, and further along on the same side is Bethel United Church.

36. Church Road c.1905. The large building on the right is the Police Station, built in 1881, adjoining Northcote Road. St. Georges church tower is in the distance.

37. The free library with its imposing iron gates. This is the original building, and has since been replaced by a new purpose-built building, on the same site.

38. This view is looking towards the city from St. Georges Fountain. The tram is about to take the right fork towards Hanham c.1939.

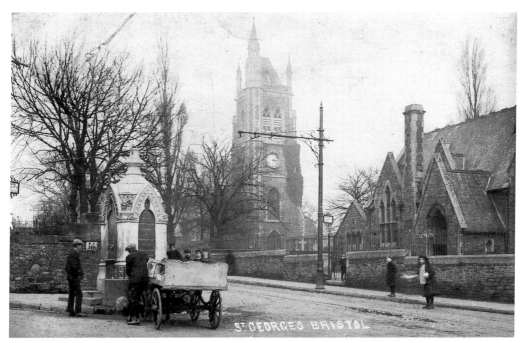

39. St. Georges Church and the fountain at the fork for Kingswood and Hanham. The William Butler Fountain was erected on the site of the Don John Cross, the boundary of the Kingswood Forest.

40. A view of the Butler Fountain, taken further back in Church Road. The divide of the tram lines clearly showing.

ST. GEORGE

41. The original church of St. George erected in 1756, and rebuilt in 1846. In 1878 it was burnt down. The tower and church were rebuilt and completed in 1879. It was finally demolished in 1976.

42. St. Georges Post Office, no.1 Clouds Hill Road, adjoining Post Office Lane and St. Georges Church of England School. The tower of St. Georges Church can be seen. This postcard was postally used in April 1909.

43. Tram no.135, passing the turning for Whiteway Road, in Clouds Hill Road, en route for Old Market in August 1939.

44. Hudds Hill Road, joins Whiteway Road, near the junction with the main road, and connects at the far end with Ventnor Road. c.1910.

45. A Whitsuntide procession heading towards Kingswood, in Two Mile Hill. The shop behind the second banner was built in 1890. It is on the corner of Rodney Road.

46. Two Mile Hill in the direction of Kingswood c.1926. The Rose and Crown Inn was built in 1905, on the corner of Birchells Green Road. Opposite a horse pulling a cart carrying a tar boiler is emerging from Cuckoo Lane.

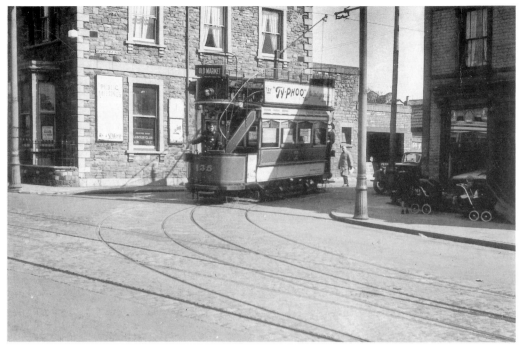

47. Summerhill Road towards Hanham, just below the turning for Hanham, Beaconsfield Road joins the main road in Church Road, tram no. 135 having just left the Beaconsfield Road Depot.

48. Large double bay villas in Glebe Road c.1908. This road is on the right hand side on entering Summerhill Road, and opposite St. Georges Fountain.

ST. GEORGE

49. This advertising postcard of the Pied Horse Hotel, in Summerhill Road, surrounding a picture of Will Hands, the proprietor, are views of the front of the hotel, the public bar, the private bar and the smoke room.

50. The Avenue, a continuation of Beaufort Road, with Jubilee Road the turning on the right. The Avenue bends left in the middle distance, and joins the main road at Summerhill Road.

ST. GEORGE

51. A class of Standard VII boys of Air Balloon Hill School, taken outside their school in 1936. The school is in Hillside Road, a turning off of Air Balloon Hill.

52. The Iron Church c.1902-03, has long since disappeared, and houses now cover the grass area. The road in the distance Nags Head Hill, the Air Balloon Tavern on the left and Mount Pleasant Chapel 1879, directly above the point of the Iron Church.

53. Tram no.124 at the top of Nags Head Hill, about to descend towards St. George and the city, en route for Old Market. The photograph was taken on April 17th 1939.

54. The arrival of the Lord Mayor to witness the laying of the foundation stone of the Wesleyan Memorial Methodist Church, on June 7th 1903. This view at Whites Hill in Bryants Hill, the church is near the junction with Kingsway.

ST. GEORGE

55. On down Bryants Hill from picture 54, by the lamp post is Pear Tree Lane, adjoining Pear Tree House built in 1882. This view c.1908.

HANHAM

56. An early view of Hanham, showing the police station with its large porch on the right. Postcard published in the "Avonvale Series" and posted August 30th 1905.

57. The High Street with tram no.121 on the route to Bushy Park, Totterdown. The public house on the right is the Crown and Horse Shoe Inn. The postcard was written from Mount Hill, Hanham and the postmark is 17th August 1915.

58. The High Street with informal family groups outside the shops, the Pound Chapel beyond, on the corner of Chapel Road. This view about 1906.

59. The motor bus at Hanham c.1906. This bus connected with the tram terminus at Hanham, and served Longwell Green, Willsbridge, Bitton and Kelston.

60. Chapel Road from the High Street, tram lines visible in the foreground. The boys are stood outside Pound Ebenezer Sunday School opened in 1880. The Methodist Chapel is on the right between the cottages, c.1905.

61. Further along the High Street from the Pound Chapel, a tram about to enter the single track towards the Hanham terminus. The postcard was written from Hanham and posted September 15th 1914.

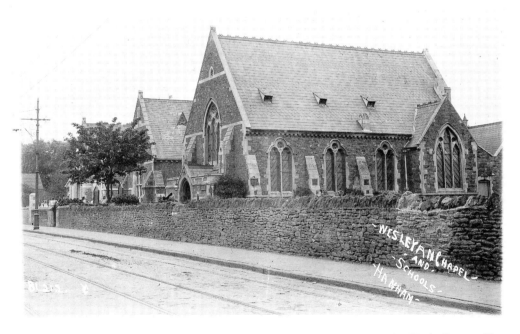

62. The Wesleyan Chapel and schools opposite Victoria Road in the High Street. The postcard was postally used on August 31st 1910.

63. The High Street looking towards Longwell Green. A tram is about to leave the tram terminus for Old Market. The double fronted entrance of Bristol Tramway and Carriage Co. Ltd., is on the right, formerly owned by W.J. Bence motor service. This view April 17th 1939.

64. This view is in the opposite direction of illustration 63, towards the centre of Hanham. The car on the left has the registration number VP 6151, and opposite behind the horse and cart a petrol tanker makes a delivery to the B.P. Garage. The photograph is by Hepworth.

CHRIST CHURCH HANHAM.

65. Christ Church was built on land donated by Mr. Whittucks in 1840, in Church Road off of Memorial Road. In 1841 a school room was opened adjoining the Church. The Church was consecrated by Bishop Monk on October 18th 1842. Mr. Barrow preached to a full congregation.

THE VICARAGE HANHAM.

66. Christ Church vicarage surrounded by extensive grounds. This postcard was posted in 1912. Today a modern vicarage has been built nearer the road.

67. The main Hanham to Longwell Green road, from the fields, which are now covered by houses in Grange Avenue, Whittucks Road area. Hanham Baptist Church, and houses between Albert Road and Hanbury Close can be seen in the distance. This postcard was postally used in 1914.

68. Hanham Baptist Church looking towards the centre of Hanham. The view is relatively unchanged today, except for the Baptist Chapel which has been rebuilt with a modern frontage.

69. Hanham Grange is in Hanham Close just off the High Street. This view is from when the Grange was surrounded by fields, the High Street is beyond the trees. This house is built on the site of a former house after 1840, when bought by Squire Whittucks. In later years one of several owners were the Bristol Brass and Copper Company.

70. Hanham Men's Adult School, a group taken c.1905. The banner behind says "God Bless our Adult School".

71. Hanham Hall when surrounded by fields. It is a hospital today in Whittucks Road. The road was named after Squire Whittuck, who was once owner of Hanham Hall. He died in 1849.

72. An early view of the River Avon at Hanham. Postally used in March 1905, the writer of the postcard mentions a trip up the river, and describes this "as a pretty view".

73. The pond at Hanham Green, in Abbots Road, next to Callingwood House. The cows are from Bickley Farm further along the road. The postcard was postally used in 1908.

74. The two small girls stand on the green, where the roads divide c.1906. The left road towards Sally on the Barn, and right is Mill Lane in the direction of the River Avon at Hanham Mills.

75. Hanham Court and St. George Church in Mill Lane. An earlier building on this site was given to Keynsham Abbey. The Creswicke family had long associations with the court, members of the family lived there for over 200 years.

76. Court Farm is situated at the end of Court Farm Road. The Barn was named "Sally on the Barn" because of the statue of "Sally" on top of the central tower. A delightful rural view. This postcard was postally used in 1913.

77. Hanham Mills, the Lock and Weir Inn facing the River Avon. Behind the cottages further along the tow path are rocks from the former quarries. This postcard postally used in 1906.

78. From the tow path at Hanham Mills the Chequers Inn, and further along the Lock and Weir Inn. This tow path extends along the river past Conham through to Crews Hole.

79. The River Avon, the weir crossing at this point, all boats navigating the river have to enter the lock near the right bank.

80. The footpath to Hanham Ferry which closed in 1940 and which used to cross the river beyond the Chequers Inn. The ferry connected to the footpaths to Keynsham.

81. Hanham Lock c.1910. The horse drawn barge named "Blanche" was owned by Thatcher Bros. quarry owners. They had the vessel to convey their stone, and it was named after their sister.

82. These cottages on the tow path beyond the Lock and Weir Inn, facing the weir.

83. A pleasure boat, the "Queen", hired to take convalescing soldiers on a cruise to Hanham Mills during the 1914-18 war. The boat was owned by F.A. Ashmead & Son, tug owners, at Netham Lock, Netham Road.

84. This view is taken from the Quarry Rocks, towards Hanham Lock, with the fields beyond in the direction of Keynsham. This postcard was posted on the 8th August 1941.

HANHAM

Bees' Tea Gardens, Hanham.

C. S. & Co., B.

85. Bee's Tea Gardens were founded in 1846, a favourite stop by pleasure boats from Bristol Bridge, or by the ferry boats between Conham and St. Anne's Park. The postcard was posted from Hanham on May 28th 1904.

86. The Ariel Rowing Club, later known as Avon Rowing Club, was founded in 1909. The boathouse is on the St. Anne's side by Conham ferry. This postcard was postally used in August 1907.

INDEX